When Trouble Shows Up

Seeing God's Transforming Love

Robert D. Jones

New
Growth
Press

www.newgrowthpress.com

New Growth Press, Greensboro, NC 27404
www.newgrowthpress.com

All Scripture quotations, unless otherwise indicated are taken from
the *Holy Bible,* New International Version®, NIV®. Copyright ©
1973, 1978, 1984, 2011 by Biblica, Inc. Used by permission. All
rights reserved worldwide.

Cover Design: Faceout books, faceout.com
Typesetting: Lisa Parnell, lparnell.com

ISBN-10: 1-939946-43-3
ISBN-13: 978-1-939946-43-0

Library of Congress Cataloging-in-Publication Data
Jones, Robert D., 1959–
  When trouble shows up : seeing God's transforming love / Robert
D. Jones. — First [edition].
     pages cm
  Includes bibliographical references and index.
  ISBN 978-1-939946-43-0 (alk. paper)
  1. Suffering—Religious aspects—Christianity. 2. Consolation.
I. Title.
  BV4909.J655 2013
  248.8'6—dc23   2013024386

Printed in Canada

21 20 19 18 17 16 15 14   2 3 4 5 6

Nicole's marriage to Dan began with a beautiful wedding where they expressed their love and commitment to each other in front of family and friends. Nicole looked forward to the rest of her life with the man of her dreams. But in recent months Dan's interest in Nicole faded rapidly. He started to spend more time at work, less time with Nicole, and no time at church. When Nicole tried to ask Dan why he had withdrawn from her and God, he responded with anger, defensiveness, and more withdrawal. Nicole's dream was becoming a nightmare, and she slipped into a deep depression. Doubts about her own faith began to plague her.

Clay and Melissa were already worried about their son Joel's lack of commitment to Jesus, but the high school vice principal's call floored them. Joel was failing two classes and had been suspended for three days after a fistfight with another student. Clay and Melissa were ashamed of Joel's behavior and anxiously wondered where his life was headed.

Based on their initial meeting Ryan enthusiastically embraced his new boss's commitment to excellence and stepped up his own work efforts. But the boss soon proved to be critical, controlling, and demanding. At their next meeting he said, "To be honest, Ryan, I am disappointed with your output and I'm not sure you are a good fit for our company. Let's give it two weeks to see if you can turn a corner." Ryan was angry—at the new boss, at himself, and even at God—and he felt helpless and hopeless in the face of his impending termination.

We all react differently when trouble shows up. When life goes wrong, some people struggle with depression and doubts like Nicole, others with fear and embarrassment like Melissa and Clay, and still others with the anger and hopelessness that Ryan experienced. Take a moment to ask yourself how you respond to trouble and hardship. You might notice that Nicole, Melissa, Clay, and Ryan, despite their different reactions, had something in common: the same fundamental faith questions. The same questions we all ask when we face hardships:

Where is God in all this?
Does he really love me?
Does he care?
How can I be sure that he cares for me?
Why is he allowing this?
What's he up to?
Is he punishing me for something I've done?
How can I see and know his love during this
    hardship?

While it is clear from Scripture that suffering is not part of God's design for the world and thus is never inherently "good," it is also clear that God uses even the difficult circumstances of our lives for his redemptive purposes. This means that, for the people of God, pain and suffering are never the final word in their lives. The Bible loudly and repeatedly declares God's love for those who belong to Jesus. For example, Romans 8 assures us that even amid the hardest adversity, God loves us.

Who shall separate us from the love of Christ?
Shall trouble or hardship or persecution or famine
or nakedness or danger or sword? As it is written:
"For your sake we face death all day long;
we are considered as sheep to be slaughtered."
No, in all these things we are more than
conquerors through him who loved us. For I am
convinced that neither death nor life, neither
angels nor demons, neither the present nor the
future, nor any powers, neither height nor depth,
nor anything else in all creation, will be able to
separate us from the love of God that is in Christ
Jesus our Lord. (8:35–39)

Certainly the apostle's list covers the kinds of trouble that Nicole, Melissa, Clay, and Ryan faced—the same hardships you face. Yet even when you know that God has promised to be with you through all kinds of troubles, the "how" questions still remain:

How does God display his love for you when
you face hardships?
How does God use trouble to accomplish his
loving purposes in your life?

These are important questions to consider. Seeing all the ways that God shows his love to you in hardship will not erase your trouble, but it will strengthen your faith, which is of greater worth than gold. And when your faith is strengthened, your hope and your love will also be strengthened. That's how God does his transforming work in us. Let's look at seven ways God lovingly meets you in the midst of your suffering. As a memory aid, I call them the *Seven E's*. Consider each one and ask the Holy Spirit to help you see where God is now at work in your life, transforming you through his love and encouragement in the midst of your trouble.

1. God Lovingly Uses Your Troubles to *Enhance* Your Relationship with Him

While times of trial can certainly tempt us to turn away from God, his invitation to come near to him can also become more precious and appealing. We often become more God-conscious in the face of trouble, and we frequently seek his face with greater fervency. Perhaps you have already noticed this at work in your life. Before trouble showed up, you were coasting a bit in your Christian life, but now you see your need for God and you are turning to him every day for help, for faith, for comfort, for strength. But perhaps you have seen the opposite dynamic at work as well. You have responded to trouble with discouragement and unbelief. Our troubles can either push us away from God or push us toward him.

Two Israelite kings demonstrated this striking contrast when they both faced the threat of military annihilation. In 2 Chronicles 28:22 we read, "In his time of trouble King Ahaz became even more unfaithful to the LORD." Yet in 2 Chronicles 33:12 we read a different response from King Manasseh: "In his distress he sought the favor of the LORD his God and humbled himself greatly before the God of his ancestors." For Ahaz, his hardship became an occasion for greater ungodliness; he turned *away* from God. For Manasseh, his similar trial became an occasion for repentance; he turned *to* God.

You can see God's love at work in your life when, instead of turning away from God in trouble, you turn toward him for help. We see this Godward perspective throughout the Psalms. The psalmists don't hide their hardships. Enemies rise against them, friends betray them, competitors plot against them, illnesses burden them, earthquakes shake their world, and, worst of all, God sometimes seems silent.

Consider Psalm 3:1–2. In the midst of his many attackers, David turns to God—not away from him—and his faith deepens and matures:

> Lord, how many are my foes! How many rise up against me!
> Many are saying of me, "God will not deliver him."

How does David respond? In verses 3–4 he draws near to God:

> But you, Lord, are a shield around me, my glory, the One who lifts my head high.
> I call out to the Lord, and he answers me from his holy mountain.

David's prayer provides both hope and an example to follow. Whether our suffering is chronic or acute, we can know God's love and experience a deepening relationship with our Savior. Difficulties don't doom us; they invite us to come to our Lord. If we will listen, they call us to pray, to read Scripture, and to worship Christ. Even your act of reading this minibook or seeking your pastor's help demonstrates this dynamic. Discover for yourself the truth of David's words, "I sought the LORD, and he answered me; he delivered me from all my fears" (Psalm 34:4). While the trial may remain, so does God's love and his invitation to draw near to him.

Nicole faced depression and doubts after her husband turned away from her. She felt the slippage in her soul. But God used Psalm 3 to awaken her. Her disappointment with Dan drove her back to Jesus and to seeing that her primary identity was being God's daughter, not Dan's wife. While Dan didn't change, Nicole did. Her troubled marriage became the soil for renewed communion with Jesus as she accepted his invitation to "approach God's throne of grace with confidence, so that we may receive mercy and find grace to help us in our time of need" (Hebrews 4:16). Nicole turned to Christ and found his help in her time of need. Despite her troubled marriage, her faith and trust in God grew.

If you are struggling with unbelief in the face of your troubles, like Nicole you can turn to Jesus and tell him all about your struggles. He already knows what's in your heart, but he would like to hear it from you. The Psalms were not written in a day, but express a process of learning about God's goodness in trouble.

You can start that process right now by turning to Christ, turning away from unbelief, and asking for his help.

Ask yourself the following questions:[1] In what ways might God lovingly use your troubles to deepen your relationship with him? What is stopping you from turning to Jesus now and asking for mercy and help in your time of need? Write out a prayer telling Jesus all about your troubles and your sorrows, and ask him for help.

2. God Lovingly Uses Your Trouble to Help You *Experience* Christ's Sufferings

Suffering reminds us that Jesus also suffered hardships. It helps us to understand better his suffering and draws us closer to him in what the Bible calls a "participation in his suffering." Whatever trouble you face, be assured that Jesus himself faced even greater trouble when he was here on earth. "For we do not have a high priest who is unable to empathize with our weaknesses, but we have one who has been tempted in every way, just as we are . . ." (Hebrews 4:15).

Think about the apostle Paul's goals in Philippians 3:10, "I want to know Christ—yes, to know the power of his resurrection and participation in his sufferings, becoming like him in his death." Think about those desires. "I want to know Christ"—and the believer in Jesus says Yes! And I want to know "the power of his resurrection"—and the believer says Yes! And I want to know a "participation in his sufferings"—but our throat freezes. We find that third Yes! too difficult to utter. Perhaps we are even tempted to plead with God, "Lord, how about two out of three?" We long to know Jesus and his resurrection power; we shy away from tasting the misery of his suffering and death.

But we will experience suffering in this broken world—and what a comfort that our Savior has as well. Have you felt bypassed or dismissed? So did Jesus. Hear his cry in Matthew 23:37, "Jerusalem, Jerusalem, you who kill the prophets and stone those sent to you, how often I have longed to gather your children together, as a hen gathers her chicks under her wings, and you were not willing." In a parallel account Luke records Jesus's tears, "As he approached Jerusalem and saw the city, he wept over it" (Luke 19:41). Have you experienced rejection? So did Jesus. He came to his own people and even they did not receive him (John 1:11). Have you felt alone or even abandoned? So did Jesus. After pledging their loyalty, his three closest friends fell asleep as he suffered in Gethsemane, and all of his apostles fled after his arrest (Mark 14:27–52).

We feel something of Jesus's heartbreak when those we love refuse our Savior. As Clay and Melissa reflected on these passages and their son's spiritual condition, they felt a special kinship with their Savior. With the Spirit's help, they were able to voice to God a similar lament for their son Joel that Jesus expressed about Jerusalem. But they also felt some measure of the grief and angst that the Lord feels not only for Joel, but also for them when they fail to follow the Lord. While their son had grieved them, they realized that too often they also had grieved God.

Maybe you lost your job due to an economic downturn or unjust termination. Maybe you experienced mistreatment from church leaders or were forced to resign a church ministry. Maybe you were divorced by a spouse who broke his vow to love, honor, and cherish you. Maybe you desire to be married but you've been bypassed by men or women who use unbiblical dating criteria. In each case, at least in some small way, your rejection or mistreatment parallels Jesus's sufferings. Because Christ has suffered on our behalf, even to the point of death, we are assured that none of our suffering will be wasted, but will be used for God's redemptive purposes. "'I have told you these things, so that in me you may have peace. In this world you will have trouble. But take heart! I have overcome the world'" (John 16:33).

Ask yourself: Write down one way your suffering is bringing you to "participate" in Jesus's sufferings. How might your troubles help you to understand better Jesus's suffering for you? How does this change your perspective on your troubles?

3. God Lovingly Uses Your Hardships to *Expose* Your Remaining Sin

In the eyes of the Old Testament people of Israel, their forty years of desert wandering was miserable, a life of physical hardship and spiritual confusion. But in the eyes of God it had a far greater purpose. "Remember how the LORD your God led you all the way in the wilderness these forty years, to humble and to test you in order to know what was in your heart, whether or not you would keep his commands" (Deuteronomy 8:2). God consistently saw in their hearts a mixture of faith and unbelief. That same mix exists in our own hearts, even today. Like the Israelites, God often leads us through adversity to uncover our remaining sin.

Thankfully, Jesus Christ, the greater Son of God—the true Israel—relived a similar temptation. Led by the Spirit into the desert, Jesus endured forty days of fasting and satanic attack. Where God's son Israel failed, God's incarnate Son Jesus succeeded. Where we have failed, Jesus—our substitute, our righteousness, and our redeemer—has succeeded in our place.

Ryan experienced God's loving refinement in the face of his new boss's critical attitudes and threatening words. Ryan had drawn comfort from Romans 8:28, "And we know that in all things God works for the good of those who love him, who have been called according to his purpose." He had been a Christian for many years and had heard this verse frequently quoted. Based on this verse Ryan was confident that his boss would soften and he would retain his job.

Yet Ryan failed to understand what God is really saying in this verse. While it assures us that God uses trials not only for his glory but also for our good—a truth that many sufferers may forget—Romans 8:28 is not a blank check for us to define the "good." We are not free to insert whatever wished-for outcome we might want, even good things like job stability or job improvement for Ryan. The "For" in verse 29 explains the "good" in verse 28: "For those God foreknew he also predestined to be conformed to the image of his

Son, that he might be the firstborn among many brothers and sisters." God's purpose—his loving purpose, as the rest of Romans 8 tells us—is to make us increasingly like his Son Jesus. God was using this hardship for Ryan's good (v. 28), and that good is Christlikeness (v. 29). Among many possible good results, God prioritizes our own growth in Christlike character and maturity as the highest good. This greatest good trumps all other goods, including our situational improvement or circumstantial relief.

As Ryan began to understand what Romans 8:28 really promised, it led him to ask a different question: how might God be using my work troubles to make me more like Jesus? With the Lord's help Ryan confessed his anger. He realized that he too struggled with being critical, controlling, and demanding. As Ryan meditated on Galatians 5:22–23, God convicted him of failing to display the fruit of the Spirit toward his boss. Ryan repented, sought God's forgiveness, and asked his boss to forgive him for his bad attitude.

The Lord also used Ryan's unjust boss to expose some areas of insubordination. Ryan spent time studying 1 Peter 2:13–25, Ephesians 6:5–8, and Romans 13:1–6, learning what God's Word teaches about submitting to people in authority, even those who wrong us. The God of amazing love used the hardship Ryan hated to expose the sin that God hated so that Ryan could repent and know the greater joys of forgiveness and growing holiness.

Ryan did lose his job—Romans 8:28 was not the blank check he hoped for. But he grew in his love for

God and others. Although this was not the help he initially wanted from God, Ryan, from the perspective of his current job where he supervises many employees, says, "I couldn't do the job I have now if God hadn't shown me then how critical and demanding I am and my difficulties with submitting to authority."

Ask yourself: In what ways has God lovingly used your troubles to expose where you go wrong? Can you think of one area of sin in your life that your suffering has exposed? If you haven't already, turn to Jesus and confess your sins so that you can experience the joy of repentance and the freedom of forgiveness.

4. God Lovingly Uses Your Troubles to *Engage* You in the Body of Christ

Trials can easily tempt us to withdraw from others and to handle our suffering alone. However, when we withdraw, we isolate ourselves from a vital source of help and hope. What hardship provides is a real-life opportunity to draw closer to our God-given brothers and sisters in our local church. It can lead us to depend on each other—not in desperate, codependent, "clingy" ways, but to deeply support, serve, and pray for one another amid the hard times.

Two passages from Paul's letters express this dynamic. In Romans 12:15, the apostle urges us to "rejoice with those who rejoice" and to "mourn with those who mourn." We readily embrace the first reality. In times of joy we want our friends to celebrate with us. But mourning with those who mourn presents a challenge. Instead of seeking help from others, we sometimes isolate ourselves, even from those who can help.

Or consider 1 Corinthians 12:26, part of Paul's extended metaphor of the church as a body and each believer as an indispensable body member: "If one part suffers, every part suffers with it; if one part is honored, every part rejoices with it." When a church member bears a heavy burden alone, that believer or that church (or both) have failed to live out this biblical vision.

In his classic work, *Life Together*, Dietrich Bonhoeffer captures this reality. "The physical presence of other Christians," he writes, "is a source of incomparable joy and strength to the believer." Citing the examples of Paul and John longing to be with other believers (1 Thessalonians 3:10; 2 Timothy 1:4; 2 John 12), Bonhoeffer continues, "The prisoner, the sick person, the Christian in exile sees in the companionship of a fellow Christian a physical sign of the gracious presence of the triune God. Visitor and visited in loneliness recognize in each other the Christ who is present in the body. . . ."[2]

The sad reality is that during a trial we sometimes do the opposite. We pull away or wall ourselves off from others. We don't feel like taking that phone call or welcoming that visit or accepting that meal invitation, even from caring brothers and sisters in Jesus. We are embarrassed about our neediness, ashamed of our sin, or humiliated by our weakness. So we retreat. We disengage. We avoid. But God our Father calls us to a higher agenda in our suffering. He wants to extend us, stretch us, and connect us more tightly to the fellow members of our church family.

Clay and Melissa were tempted to hide Joel's problems from even their closest friends. They were so ashamed and they felt like bad parents. But they turned to their pastor, and he encouraged them to ask five people that they trusted to pray for them. So, even though it was difficult, they shared their struggles with five close friends and asked for prayer. They were amazed at how people responded. Those with children about the same age as Joel shared their own parenting struggles and some of the mistakes that their children had made. Together they learned to pray for one another and "to carry each other's burdens" (Galatians 6:2).

Ask yourself: In what ways is God lovingly using your troubles to deepen your relationship with your fellow Christians? How might God be pushing you into deeper relationships with other Christians? Do you have suffering friends that need you to help bear their burdens?

5. God Lovingly Uses Your Troubles to *Exhibit* Christ's Work in You

Few things are more encouraging to me than watching fellow Christians demonstrate their faith through the way they express wisdom, love, and grace in hard circumstances. Seeing their faith, stirs my faith. Your trouble right now is also an opportunity for people around you to see the light of Jesus Christ in you.

Jesus explains this truth with two vivid illustrations: "You are the salt of the earth. . . . You are the light of the world. . . . In the same way, let your light shine before others, that they may see your good deeds and glorify your Father in heaven" (Matthew 5:13–16). Jesus's disciples function as salt and light in a fallen world.

While some people use these salt and light images to support broader social, cultural, or political causes, the context of Jesus's words points in a different direction. The preceding verses (5:1–12, the Beatitudes) picture God's people suffering personal, evil opposition. Jesus is not addressing how to preserve or transform a decaying society through social, cultural, or political programs, but how to handle persecution from unbelievers because of our allegiance to Jesus. His salt and light images encourage Christian disciples to display his grace when facing such mistreatment. In an ungodly world, God's people radiate God.

That leads us to this sobering question: what are onlookers—our friends, family, children, and coworkers—learning about our Savior by observing how we handle tough situations? Trials grant us unparalleled opportunities to honor and spotlight God—to show others the real difference he makes in our lives. This might seem like an overwhelming or even oppressive task, especially when you are already feeling overwhelmed by the struggle itself. But taking the time to think through how you can make God known in the midst of difficulty can help you remember God's true character and purposes. In this way you are reminding yourself of the truth of the gospel, even as you seek to make Christ known to others.

Nicole learned these truths in the laboratory of a difficult marriage. Eventually Dan left her—without even really saying why. Abandoned, she struggled with depression and anger. Through Christ-centered counseling, Nicole was again able to re-anchor her identity as God's daughter to freshly "know and rely on the love God has for us" (1 John 4:16), and to depend on him as her "refuge and strength, an ever-present help in trouble" (Psalm 46:1). As she prayed and meditated on God's Word, his Spirit strengthened her—so much so that her children, friends, coworkers (Christian and non-Christian), and pastor marveled at her faith, the way she weathered this marital storm with grace, wisdom, and stability. Nicole didn't feel like a hero of the faith, but her unshaken faith in God despite her disappointing circumstances became a source of spiritual encouragement to all who knew her.

Many people have come to saving faith in Jesus through watching the soul-stirring ways that Christians they know have handled adversity. God's kingdom purposes extend beyond our personal walk with God. God may be using your hardship to help other sufferers follow Jesus too. Many Christians have grown in spiritual maturity as they have watched other Christians deal gracefully with suffering.

Ask yourself: In what ways is God lovingly using your troubles to show others the Spirit-given life and light of Jesus that you have and they need? List some ways you have been encouraged by others as you have watched them display faith in their troubles.

6. God Lovingly Uses Your Troubles to *Equip* You for Wiser, More Compassionate Ministry

If you struggle with a personal problem, what kind of person would you turn to for counsel? You would want someone who genuinely cares about you and sincerely wants to help. You would want someone you could trust, a person who would maintain confidentiality. And you would want someone who knows God's Word and who can help you understand and apply it wisely to your struggle.

But one more quality might also attract you. You would love to talk with someone who faced similar struggles and learned to handle them God's way. You would value a person who not only has "been there," but who has also managed the trial well and who can model how to deal with it God's way.

This leads us to a sixth way God uses hardships to show his love and further his purposes: to equip us for wiser, more compassionate ministry. As we learn to apply God's gospel truths to our own problems, God fashions us into more effective people-helpers. Paul says in 2 Corinthians 1:3–4, "Praise be to the God and Father of our Lord Jesus Christ, the Father of compassion and the God of all comfort, who comforts us in all our troubles, so that we can comfort those in any trouble with the comfort we ourselves receive from God." Suffering by faith equips us to help others suffer faithfully.

In verse 9, Paul brought his personal testimony to his readers. In the face of death, he admitted his temptation to trust in himself more than God. But God led him through that trial—"this happened that we might not rely on ourselves but on God"—producing an apostle more fit to minister. God comforts us in our hardships so that we would not only be comforted but also comfort others.

Joel's ongoing choice not to follow Jesus weighed down Clay and Melissa. While some parents experience the joy of prodigal sons or daughters returning to the Lord in their young-adult years, sadly, this couple did not. Despite their faithful prayers, constant love, and gospel-centered counsel, Joel has not yet embraced his parents' faith. Yet God's Spirit was working powerfully in Clay and Melissa's life, enabling them to find a profound comfort from God that was not built on Joel's decision. By absorbing and rehearsing the biblical truths in this minibook, their own faith matured. Amid their pain they came to know and walk with the Lord in deeper ways. In addition, something else happened unexpectedly. Other parents in similar situations shared their struggles with Clay and Melissa and sought their prayers, support, and counsel. Together and individually Melissa and Clay were able to pray with, weep with, and encourage the hearts of three other couples with similar burdens. Without even realizing it, God was making them into those who could comfort others with the comfort they received from God.

Ask yourself: How is God lovingly using your hardships to make you a more compassionate, wise people-helper? In what ways have you received God's comfort through the ministry of others who have been comforted by God's grace in their own struggles?

7. God Lovingly Uses Your Troubles to *Elevate* Your Longing for Christ's Return

Living in a fallen world need not lead us to despair. It can stir us instead to long for something better. Consider the apostle Peter's richly expectant perspective.

> In all this you greatly rejoice, though now for a little while you may have had to suffer grief in all kinds of trials. These have come so that the proven genuineness of your faith—of greater worth than gold, which perishes even though refined by fire— may result in praise, glory and honor when Jesus Christ is revealed. (1 Peter 1:6–7)

By framing current problems in light of eternity, Peter raises our eyes. "Therefore," verse 13 concludes, "with minds that are alert and fully sober, set your hope on the grace to be brought to you when Jesus Christ is revealed at his coming." Amid afflictions, fix your hope on God's future grace found in Jesus's return.

The apostle James agrees. In James 1:12, he comforts his suffering readers, "Blessed is the one who perseveres under trial because, having stood the test, that person will receive the crown of life that the Lord has promised to those who love him." Persevering now yields a future crown.

This points to the seventh way God displays his love when we suffer: to encourage us to look forward in hope to Jesus's return. By letting us experience hardships, God helps us desire the eternal state to come—to make us people who are "looking forward to a new heaven and a new earth, where righteousness dwells" (2 Peter 3:13).

Suffering exposes the lie that the best things in life are found in *this* life, or that gaining the temporal, earthly things we lack would deeply satisfy our souls. When these lies control our minds, disaster ensues. When our possessions dwindle, our marriages hit potholes, our jobs yield thorns, our bodies deteriorate, and our earthly homes decay, these gospel promises from Peter and James rise up to overshadow our losses and guarantee greater gains.

Have you noticed that nearly every Bible passage that promises Christ's return is written to or about *suffering* Christians? Whether it is Jesus's description of his return in the Gospels, Paul's stress on the Second Coming in 1 and 2 Thessalonians, John's glorious pictures in the book of Revelation, or the words of Peter and James above, the Bible brings future-oriented hope to Christians facing afflictions. For those who suffer in this life, God promises a better life to come.

Of course, this requires eyes of faith to see God and these unseen provisions, lest this expectation be merely some pie-in-the-sky dream, an escapist fantasy born out of desperation. It requires us to cultivate an acquired taste to see and dwell with God. May his Spirit alter our taste buds—our affections and values—from the earthly comforts and relief we crave to the richer, eternal delights he guarantees.

Ask yourself: In what ways might God lovingly use your hardships to heighten your desire for Christ's return and the new heaven and earth he will bring? How does the Bible's eternal perspective help you look differently—in better ways—at your present problems?

Conclusion

Is suffering a good thing? No. It is a bad thing, not part of God's pre-fallen world. But the God of grace can bring good things from bad things. He reverses the curse and redeems a fallen world. He takes sinful, suffering people, displays his love, and makes them glorious. Whatever your specific hardship, you can be certain of these truths.

As you move forward, select one hardship you face, review the above Seven-E truths, consider the loving biblical purposes that might apply to your hardship, and talk to God about them. (Composing a written prayer journal would be ideal.) Ask him to reassure you of his love and to show you the good purposes he might be trying to cultivate in you through your trials. Ask him to give you a heart that wants to know him better and to grow in his grace so that the psalmist's testimony can become yours: "It was good for me to be afflicted so that I might learn your decrees" (Psalm 119:71).

Finally, look for opportunities to come alongside others who face difficult circumstances, even if their circumstances differ from yours. Enter their world, understand their struggle, and gently bring them the Christ-centered hope that this minibook offers.

Let me close with this reassurance. While many factors can make a trial endurable, nothing is more important than knowing that God loves you, that he is with you in the hardship, that he is in control, and that he has loving purposes for you in allowing this trouble to show up. Your suffering is not wasted. He is using your trial to produce something beneficial for you and in you. He redeems you not only in your initial conversion but also in ongoing, daily ways. Knowing that there are positive, love-driven, divine purposes can strengthen your soul and propel you through each trouble you face.

Endnotes

1. You can use these "Ask Yourself" questions (found after each of the Seven E's) as an individual or in a small group setting for personal reflection, application, discussion, prayer, etc. You can focus on past or present hardships. I sometimes ask a counselee to study and meditate on the verses in this minibook and then compose a written prayer to God after each "E." You can also ask how you have seen these positive purposes lived out by others who have handled hardships in godly ways.

2. Dietrich Bonhoeffer, *Life Together*, John W. Doberstein, trans. (San Francisco: Harper & Row, 1954), 19.